# Honkytonk Heroes

"Country" has changed. And that's what this book is about. For country music in the last forty years has reflected the changing face of America. The music's metamorphosis parallels the transition of a generation that made the switch from rural to urban, from poor to affluent. In these photographs by Raeanne Rubenstein are all the elements of that peculiar mix that is country music today—the legacies from the past, the Kings and Queens of country, the New Wave, the outlaws, the Opry faithful. Country music might have tried to retain some of its back-porch simplicity, but the times have changed and "country" has changed with them. The entertainers featured in this book account for the vast bulk of the country music now being heard on the airwaves of this continent.

Today country music is everywhere, and it has incorporated styles of music from everywhere: from black slaves, from Cajuns, from Mexicans and Hawaiians. And in the last ten years, many early rock singers have returned to their country music origins. Country music is the music of America.

# HONKYTONK HEROES

## A Photo Album of Country Music

### Photographs by Raeanne Rubenstein

### Text by Peter McCabe

Harper & Row, Publishers / New York  Evanston  San Francisco  London

This book
is dedicated to my parents,
Sylvia Rubenstein and Isidore Rubenstein

Designed by Dorothy Schmiderer

Library of Congress Cataloging in Publication Data

Rubenstein, Raeanne.
  Honkytonk heroes.

    1.  Country musicians—United States—Pictorial works.
I.  McCabe, Peter, 1945–      II.  Title.
ML87.R8      779'.2      74–20406
ISBN 0–06–012892–5
ISBN 0–06–012893–3 pbk.

75 76 77 78 79 10 9 8 7 6 5 4 3 2 1

# Contents

Acknowledgments      vi

Introduction: "Country Has Changed."      1

1: The Telecaster Cowboy Outlaws      13

2: The Kings and Queens of Country      33

3: The New Wave      59

4: Plastic Rose Country Dream Living      97

5: Good Ole Boys (and a Few Good Ole Gals)      119

A Note from the Photographer      151

# Acknowledgments

With special thanks to Bonnie Garner, Dan Beck, Mary Ann McCready, Judy Wray, Teresa Dodson, Beth Pate, Emily Mitchell and everyone at C.B.S. in Nashville. Ron Oberman, Bill Williams, Bob Beckham, Chris Black, Melva Matthews, Frank Jones, Howard Bloom, Sam Lovullo, Chris Forte, J. Clarke Thomas, Gene Bear, Dann Moss, Moony Lynn, John Brown, Chet Atkins, Bill Ivey, Jim Wagner, Lester Vanadore, Tim Wipperman, Leo Zabelin, Jim Halsey, Ren Grevatt, Peter Rudge, Bill Carter, Bob Levinson, Bill Langstroth, Anne Murray, Ed Giedt, Chuck Glaser, Captain Midnight, Mel Shestack, JR Young, Elisabeth Jakab, Lindsay Maracotta, Neil Reshan and Marci Robbins, of Nikon Professional Services.

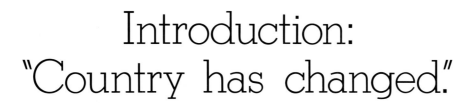

# Introduction:
# "Country has changed."

It was a blustery fall night in Chicago, with a saber-toothed wind whipping in off Lake Michigan, but the weekend weather forecast for Tennessee was optimistic, and the rich Georgia tones of the honey blonde behind the Amtrak counter had already whetted my appetite for red clay, antebellum mansions, country-fried steak and fatback-flavored vegetables. With these thoughts in mind, I'd been trying to doze off on one of the hard wooden seats of the Union Station waiting room when the old man woke me up.

"You goin' south, mister?"

"I'm gonna Nashville," I said without further elaboration, but he was not easily discouraged.

"I'm gonna Memphis. Takin' a later train than you. Least Memphis is my first stop, then I takes a bus to a little town in Arkansas you probably ain't heard of. Hickory Ridge is its name."

He cleared his throat and made his pitch. "Mister, I sure hate to ask you this, but I just sank my last few dollars into this fare. Now I wouldn't normally ask a fella this, but . . . well, I could sure use a cup of coffee."

He wasn't your ordinary city speed-freak panhandler, probably didn't know the meaning of the phrase "spare change." An old battered suitcase rested between his knees, and the collar was coming adrift from his worn Pendleton shirt. I handed him a quarter and offered him a cigarette, and he accepted both. He crossed the waiting room to a concession stand and bought himself a coffee, stirred it ceremoniously, then came back and sat next to me.

"Mighty kind of you, mister." He wiped a few drips of liquid from his two-day stubble with one sweep of his sleeve. "You make this trip often?"

"First time for me. Just felt like riding the train for a change."

"Oh, I ride the rails all the time," he told me. "Bin comin' to Chicago off and on for more than thirty years. But I always go back after a while. This town ain't easy on a country boy—not that the country's specially easy on a country boy these days. Country's changed. There's places near my home I don't recognize no more. South ain't what it used to be."

A departure announcement came over the loudspeaker.

"That's your train, mister," said the old man. "What's that they called it? The Floridean? Well, I niver. You sure ain't riding the Southbound no more. Fact is, you ain't ever gonna know what it was like to ride the Southbound."

We said good-bye, and I boarded my train. Sitting next to me was a hillbilly family from the North Side. The father introduced them all as the train pulled out. . . . "My wife, Loretta, young Johnny, Sue. Sure hope these kids don't keep you awake tonight. They're pretty darn worked up over this trip. We goin' to Florida—to Disney World!"

It was then that it hit me. I was riding the Southbound to Disney World!

I looked out of the window as we rolled past the freight cars . . . all the familiar names . . . Erie & Lackawanna, Gulf Mobile & Ohio, Rock Island Line . . . then suddenly Japanese Container Freight.

The old man was right. The country has changed.

And that's what this book is about. For country music in the last forty years has reflected the changing face of America. The music's metamorphosis parallels the transition of a generation that made the switch from rural to urban, from poor to affluent. In these photographs by Raeanne Rubenstein are all the elements of that peculiar mix that is country music today—the legacies from the past, the kings and queens of country, the New Wave, the outlaws, the Opry faithful. Country music might have tried to retain some of its back-porch simplicity, but times have changed and country has changed with them. And no matter what your mental picture of country musicians may be, it is the entertainers featured in this book who account for the vast bulk of the country music heard on the airwaves of this continent today.

But first we should look back a bit to a heritage that is hundreds of years old, older than the United States itself. For it was the Scotch-Irish settlers, bringing their traditional songs and instruments to the Appalachian mountains, to the South and later to the West, who gave birth to what eventually became known as country music. These settlers preserved many of the songs and sounds of the old country, as is made evident by so many folk or country ballads now called American which have similar versions, with the same lyrics or message—cousins, you might call them—in Scotland, Ireland or England today. Even the basic style of rendition has changed little; the mournful style of, say, Roy Acuff is not all that different from that of many an Irish balladeer. But inevitably the new environment prompted new songs—new stories to tell, new tragedies to lament, new myths and legends to perpetuate—and in place of bagpipes and lutes there appeared zithers, guitars and banjos. And yet, even here there are similarities. The wail of a fiddle in a bluegrass song bears a striking resemblance to the haunting sound of Scottish bagpipes.

As the settlers spread out to the south and west, the music of Appalachia spread with them, changing form slightly in each new environment as new influences appeared. And throughout the nineteenth century and the first three decades of the twentieth this "country" music established itself as the real folk music of white rural America—forlorn lyrics about loving and leaving, heartbreak and dying, an earthy musical commentary that rang out first on the homestead back porches, then later on the jukeboxes and radios throughout the South and Appalachia. Then came the thirties and the forties, and migrations of country people spread outward, first west to California from Oklahoma and Texas, then north from Appalachia and the South to such cities as Detroit, Chicago, Cleveland, Milwaukee and Baltimore. The migrants brought their music with them; it was a sound they never outgrew even when they moved into the cities, a musical attachment to a country-life childhood, a remembrance of roots. In the urban areas they began to write songs about their new way of life, city life, though in the same country-music style, and the result was country songs about cities, such as "Dallas," "Streets of Baltimore," "Saginaw, Michigan," "New York City Blues." Lots of songs were written about the railroad, too. The railroads offered an escape, a way to go home. "Oh, how I wanna go home," sang the car worker, complaining about Detroit.

But at the same time country people moved into the cities, concrete was spreading to rural America. McDonald's, Holiday Inns and the Exxon tiger extended their limp reach into every cranny of what was formerly known as the country.. Tumbleweeds could offer little resistance to Seven-Elevens, shopping malls and diagonal parking lots. As the city and the country mingled, it was hardly surprising that some new influences began to creep into country music. It was a slow process at first, but slowly the world of country music, so tight unto itself, was forced to admit those it had always regarded as outsiders; although there is still a solid core of performers who might truthfully be called country (in that they were raised in the country, took baths in the kitchen or picked cotton for a living), there are many other "country" performers today who are more likely to have dog crap than cow dung on their fancy Frye boots.

Today country music is everywhere, and it has incorporated styles of music from everywhere: from black slaves, from Cajuns, from Mexicans and Hawaiians. It's no longer just the musical memories of Appalachian settlers; country singers have broadened their range of subjects—Jimmy Rodgers and Hank Snow sang of the railroad, the Carter Family sang industrial ballads, Gene Autry sang of the loneliness of the prairie. And in the last ten years many early rock singers who grew up country boys have returned to country music, singers such as Jerry Lee Lewis and Conway Twitty.

As the music obtained greater acceptance across a broader spectrum of society, it was easier for an entertainer to earn a lucrative living singing country songs. And in the sixties we at last saw the recognition of country as a musical "art form," considered peculiar to America, equal in the esteem in which so many intellectuals and musicologists had long held jazz. In some circles country has even become camp.

Its rise in popularity is amply illustrated by the increase in the number of radio stations playing country music full time. In 1963 there were less than 150 such stations in the United States. Today the number is over 1,000, and in the past three years alone the number has risen by more than 200. Now there is no major city in the United States which does not have a large country-music station. Of the $2 billion worth of record and tape sales in the United States last year, nearly $400 million worth—20 percent—was country. For several years the second most popular syndicated TV show (after The Lawrence Welk Show) has been the country music production Hee Haw, now marketed through more than three hundred outlets. It had had a network slot at C.B.S. until C.B.S. decided to deruralize its image. There are still some red faces at C.B.S. when that subject is mentioned, though the network redeems itself by continuing to broadcast the annual Country Music Awards show.

The awards show invariably swamps Monday-night football to draw top ratings; as a program it should interest us for what it says about country music today. If the late, great Hank Williams could have watched the last awards show, he would probably have been whirling in his grave. For one thing, he would not have recognized even the stage of the Grand Ole Opry, a stage on which he was encored six times when he first sang his immortal "Lovesick Blues" there. The Grand Ole Opry, in which membership for any singer who called himself country was once almost obligatory, was formerly housed in the Ryman Auditorium, a nineteenth-century converted tabernacle in the heart of downtown Nashville which for more than thirty years was the very pulse of country music. It has now been abandoned in favor of what is cutely called a new Grand Ole Opry House, a modern, air-conditioned, four-thousand-seat facility located ten miles east of Nashville in the heart of an amusement park called Opryland, a veritable Disneyland itself. One wonders what Hank might have thought of all those back-slapping record executives talking about charts and bullets, of country stars wearing tuxedos, of the special-effect lighting designed to project "glitter," no less, on the TV viewer's screen. Perhaps Hank might have decided that Davy Crockett had some sense after all, packing up in Tennessee and leaving for Texas.

And what would Hank have thought of the music? Well,

he would have recognized old Hank Snow, the Singin' Ranger, still wearing his toupee and singing of "big eight wheelers rolling down the track." He would have remembered Kitty Wells reminding men that "It Wasn't God Who Made Honky-Tonk Angels." And he would have recognized Loretta Lynn's voice, with its hard mountain edge, as an honest-to-God country voice. But Olivia Newton-John, "Female Entertainer of the Year," with her plum-in-the-mouth English accent? And Danny Davis, with his trumpets and trombones, calling himself country music's ambassador? Well, ole Hank might have decided that he did the right thing after all, getting out while the going was good.

But English accents, trombones, string-quartet backings and rock-accented guitar riffs are a part of country music today. Some fans resent this. Remembering what the music used to be, they complain that it's been watered down. The proponents of "modern country" claim country music has simply spread its wings and is drawing from other areas of music. The truth lies somewhere in between, but for certain the music is no longer aimed at just country people. Today it is the music of many people who have aspired to the rewards of middle-class urban life. What's more, the country entertainers might like to think of themselves as good ole boys and gals, but many of them are good ole boys and gals in Dacron and polyester crushproof clothing, living in ranchettes in the suburbs of Nashville and driving well-upholstered interior-sprung Cadillacs. They are the hub of an "industry" that turns out $400 million worth of "product" annually.

Country music is no longer a mandolin, fiddle, banjo, bass and four voices in tight harmony, clear as a Kentucky morning. Some country fans today might furiously deny any association with "hillbilly" music, though they buy the records of Johnny Cash and Tammy Wynette. It is, as we said earlier, a strange world, full of contradictions and enigmas.

This book attempts to shed some light on this country confusion by focusing on the people who make the music. After all, if you study poets as well as their work, you get a better understanding of what poetry is all about. The same applies to country music and country musicians—and make no mistake; these country songs are the "poetry" that most Americans listen to and love. And yet hard as it is to define a country song, it may be even harder to define a country singer. A lot of entertainers will conveniently borrow the label "country," hoping to score points with the country audience, when in fact they're about as country as Frank Sinatra. On the other hand, there are a lot of country boys playing in rock 'n' roll bands who are much nearer to the true spirit of country than many a Nashville record executive. Country singers do not all fit in the same mold, and neither do their songs.

However, it might be fair to say of country music in general that it is a music with Southern and rural taproots; its politics are generally conservative and patriotic; its economics are blue collar and interference by the federal government be damned; most of its older entertainers share the same views about God and the Eastern liberal elite that Richard Nixon holds, yet many of their songs acknowledge the need for an abundance of liquor from time to time to drown sorrows. Country songs demonstrate a real empathy for the working man and woman (though still in clearly defined roles), and there isn't a country singer I can immediately recall who has not sung a song about the fact that occasionally men and women have been known to share beds with other than their husbands and wives. Even here, though, there is often a moral to the tale, or if not, the issue may be left unresolved, with both parties being forced to live with an unhappy situation; this is a music that is not shy on fatalism or sentiment.

As for the people themselves, the country entertainer for the most part was born in poor or modest circumstances. He or she generally learned to play an instrument without any formal schooling, possibly with the aid of a parent or relative. They knew hard times and hard work even when they were children, and the latter is a habit that they rarely break with as they sacrifice their own comfort to travel countless hours and miles back and forth across the country to bring their music to their audience. In a word, they are dedicated, self-made men and women who know only too well that there are few pleasures that go along with poverty and so strive for as much material reward as they can achieve.

And yet they rarely forget their roots; they never rise above their audience, except materially (this is almost a golden rule they all adhere to), recognizing that any fancy airs and manners would immediately turn off their fans. But frankly, few of them want to lose their past. They may buy large, expensive houses in garish taste or install guitar-shaped swimming pools in their backyards, but that kind of behavior is accepted and, indeed, expected by the fans. It is exactly what the fan would do if he or she won a lottery or struck oil. What is more important is that the stars don't lose their taste for country-fried chicken and potato salad, baskets of which are often provided them by fans at many a country concert. (Country music's groupies are known as chicken ladies.)

It is, of course, the tendency toward outlandish embellishment which has always drawn the sneers from city sophisticates. Sudden wealth after bitter poverty is often accompanied by the need to flaunt it, and country-music styles over the years have followed some pretty wild trends. One of the earliest influences on country music was its infusion with "Western," and it was not surprising that when country singers, in generally poor rural attire of overalls, ginghams and homespun calicos, came up alongside the likes of singing cowboys like Gene Autry, who wore glamorous "Western" outfits, they felt they had to do something to make the match more equal. So in came spangles, sequins, studs, rhinestones, silks, satins, crinolines and elaborate embroidery, everything from peacock feathers to crowns and anchors. One performer, Hawkshaw Hawkins, wore a silk jacket with a golden hawk embroidered on the back. The main designer of all this embellishment is a man called Nudie, who practices what he promotes, driving a twenty-thousand-dollar custom-made Pontiac that has rams' horns on the hood and an interior embedded with eight hundred silver dollars.

It would not be entirely unfair to say that some of the crudest elements of the entertainment world have been adopted by country musicians. However, it is always this aspect of the entire scene—the outlandish garb or grotesque gimmick—which attracts the attention of the visiting Northern journalist to the exclusion of almost all other redeeming features. Nashville musicians are all too familiar with the line "I want to understand your world," only to eventually read an article about how the country folk indulge in old-fashioned, hokey, guilt-ridden cheatin' while wearing clothes that grandma wouldn't wear and talking in a style that went out before William Faulkner began writing. It's not surprising they're suspicious.

Not that the snobbery and aloofness toward country music and country people is all Northern. Nashville's aristocracy still cringes at the mere mention of what their town is most famous for. Some of country's strongest detractors are Southern boys who spent a few years at an Ivy League school; rather than conveniently forgetting their humble origins, they protest too much. Many still really love country music (once it's in your system, it's hard to work it out), but if they're driving in an open car with the radio on, they are ready to change the station at red lights.

On the other hand, successful Southern politicians have long been aware of the importance of country music to their electorate. George Wallace has always made sure that his campaign includes enough country singers to fill the stage of the Grand Ole Opry—not that there's anything phony about his appreciation of country music, since he knows nearly every major entertainer on a first-name basis and has paid a few visits to the Grand Ole Opry in his time. And country music has served quite a few Southern politicians in another way. Louisiana's former governor Jimmie Davis, for example, was elected twice, his popularity assured by the appeal of his song, "You Are My Sunshine." Even Richard Nixon, as part of his "Southern strategy," invited Johnny Cash, Merle Haggard and countless other country stars to play at the White House.

Of course, Nixon was only the latest in a long line of people who recognized that country music could reach a constituency. Country-music concerts grew out of the medicine shows, and almost any advertiser who didn't reach a rural or Southern audience by announcing his wares on a country radio station has long since gone bankrupt. Even today, despite the changes in country music, a city dweller or Northerner driving across Kansas or Alabama will hear about a vast range of products, from salves to farm implements to brands of flour, that have never previously reached his city ears. And just as the doctor on the medicine show always hired the musicians and set up the show in small communities, selling liniments, worm cure, special soaps that allowed you to keep your hair, so the sponsors of today—Martha White Flour, Ralston Purina, American Gasoline—will either buy half hours of time from the <u>Grand Ole Opry</u> show or hire the country star for TV spots. Often the song in the commercial, like Dottie West's Coke commercial, becomes a hit— "Country Sunshine." What more perfect arrangement, in the true American tradition?

It is a mistake to imagine that country was ever uncommercial. It is even more commercial today. This is a hard, tough business, and talented though a singer might be, his career will depend on one item only—having a hit song. Naturally, the process of creating this desirable commodity—and I use that term deliberately—has become sophisticated far beyond backwoods origins. The music scene in Nashville today is chock full of smart businessmen, professional recording engineers, skilled songwriters, tastemakers, hip promoters and every other kind of hustler that it takes to launch a musical theme. The country sound has been polished to a sleek, smooth shell of its former self, though consciously maintaining elements of the distinctive twang. Whether country is still country is a subject that consumes hours of discussion in Nashville, though not for aesthetic reasons; what's important is only what sells. Perhaps the present state of the art—in which traditional sounds and modern string-backed sounds both sell (largely depending on the popularity of the entertainer or the quality of the song)—is indicative of what might be the most important principle behind any record released: It must have a good catchy tune and lyrics that strike a chord in the hearts and/or minds of the listeners. But add to this the consummate skills of the Nashville producers—people like Tammy Wynette's producer, Billy Sherrill—whose stock in trade includes such items as hook lines, bridges, choruses, all of which must be just right in the modern country song. At least that is the theory; then a new boy comes out of the woods with a different idea of how things should be done, and he hits the number-one spot in the charts first time. But that's what makes the business so fascinating.

Perhaps we can define two real watersheds in the development of country music in recent years. The first was when drums were allowed onto the stage of the Grand Ole Opry, a decision that in its day was considered by the traditionalists to be little short of heretical. But it changed the face of the music. So did two other factors, which must really be considered as one: first, the death of Hank Williams in 1953; second, the ascent of Elvis Presley in 1955.

Williams has grown into a mighty legend in the more than twenty years since he died. If any singer can be said to have propagated a style of singing that has been so very basic to the modern trend of the music, it is Williams. (I know that others might argue this point and say that Jimmie Rodgers was the father of country music, but today more people imitate Williams consciously or otherwise than they do Rodgers, so I stick to my guns.) Ironically, Williams's influence hit its low point only a few years after his death. That was when rhythm and blues and country secretly married, and the resultant offspring, rock 'n' roll, personified by Elvis Presley, grew at such a rate that it almost devoured both its parents in the process. For several years, and of course even today, countless country boys who might have sung in the style of Hank Williams followed Presley, the Pied Piper, into rock 'n' roll, abandoning the music they grew up to. Those were the lean years for country, but the mournful wail and the nasal twang and the choke in the voice which were Williams's trademarks (not that his genius can ever be that simply defined in print) persisted stubbornly, and as musical tastes in the sixties and seventies drifted back toward ballads, the Williams influence began to be revived. Today it's hard to turn on a country station and not hear, in spite of the plethora of string backings that are currently in vogue, some unconscious imitation of the voice of Hank Williams.

Yet it would be naive to assume that country has come full circle. That is far from the case. The underlying elements are certainly still intact: a basic simple music and lyrics that cover the hallowed ground of love and grief, sentiment and nostalgia, preferring to deal with the emotions rather than the intellect. As we said at the beginning of this introduction, the country has changed, and the music may be cyclical in some respects, but it always builds on the past. The music has changed as the country has changed; it has spread with migrations, influencing new adherents and being influenced by new environments. It is easy to agree with the argument that the music has lost some of its flavor, to note that its innocence has diminished as the years have gone by. But perhaps what is more remarkable is the music's tenacity, the fact that in spite of business, the recording industry, charts and bullets, freeway interchanges and space travel, it still produces a gut response in the people who love it, a response that carries over from one generation to another. Better to adjust to modernity than to be its victim.

I bring up this issue once again because I feel it is almost symptomatic of the way most of us live out our lives. In our daily existence we are always making compromises in order to survive. We adapt. We aspire to new adventures, greater wealth, new ideals, a better standard. Yet we surround ourselves with the things that make us feel secure, the same things that have been the staple of our parents' existence—husbands, wives, families, houses, furniture, mementos. There's a dichotomy here, and it's a dichotomy that is reflected in the course that country music has taken, though if anything the greater emphasis rests with the traditional, the basics. Which isn't surprising. Country music and the people who make it are basic.

I recall once sitting on Roy Acuff's back porch and talking with him about this very subject—the change in country music, the new people who now liked it, the change in singing styles, new wealth, people driving to Nashville to go to Opryland rather than to the Grand Ole Opry, the old one. Didn't he secretly miss the old times and the old ways, the unaccompanied singing voice, the acoustic guitar, the crazy-quilt pattern of old American country ways, singing, joke-telling, yarn-swapping, barn dancing, reminiscing? He looked at me almost coyly, as if suspecting that I might have already made up my mind. He admitted he did miss those things, all of them. Then he said, "Well, I grew up with country people. I like country people. But when folks come here to hear this music, I don't want to see them poor and hungry. I want them to ride the Wabash Cannonball in here and fly out on a jet plane."

Like the old man said, "Country has changed."

12

# 1

# The Telecaster
# Cowboy Outlaws

After a seven-year battle with barbiturates and amphetamines, Cash quit the habit in 1968. Within two years he was host of an enormously successful TV show, and his name was a household word. This picture was taken in his dressing room behind the Ryman Auditorium during a taping of The Johnny Cash Show (Nashville, Tennessee, 1969).

"I'd run through every evil, dirty thing there is, and I didn't like it. I wanted to live!" Cash today, very much alive, outside the Columbia Records recording studio, during a session break.

In an earlier generation they might have been real outlaws. They were, after all, independent spirits who rejected the bank-clerk/factory-hand existence, just as their predecessors said no to the cottonfields and marshalling yards. The times that spawned the music on which the older ones were reared often made heroes of bad men in an age when rattling Model T's loaded down with mattresses, cardboard suitcases and hungry children headed west, on a grim retreat from the failures of the Dust Bowl. It was an age that produced and loved and immortalized the likes of John Dillinger, Bonnie Parker and Clyde Barrow.

The Country Music Outlaws. The Telecaster Cowboys, their guitars slung low like an outlaw's gun. They defy labels and categories. They don't even have much in common musically, except that they've stayed close to their individual musical roots, refusing to be led by the nose by the Tin Pan Alley cigar chompers and Burbank big shots who would have put them in tights and set them down in front of cameras, backed by rows of lush chorus girls and a string quartet. They knew that wasn't the way anymore. Nor was it necessary to brush your teeth and wear white bucks in order to impress the ladies. That's natural outlaw instinct at work there, the same kind of raw nerve that allows you to say whatever you like on stage and still have the audience respect you for it.

Johnny Cash knew what that was all about in the days when he sang about "walking the line," even though most of the time he couldn't.

"Well, folks, that's the kind of song you're gonna be hearing tonight. Now those of you who don't like it can try and get your money back."

The fans loved him for it.

Marty Robbins once said that playing the road was like robbing Wells Fargo—you rode in, took the money and rode out. Marty would know. On the honky-tonk circuit he saw enough willing hands slap down three crumpled bills just to hear him sing "El Paso." Marty also knew they loved outlaws, and he sang about them, but others, most notably Johnny Cash, Merle Haggard, Jerry Lee Lewis, Waylon Jennings, George Jones, Johnny Paycheck and Hank Williams, lived like them, at least for a while. So did the younger ones—David Allan Coe, Billy Joe

Waylon Jennings. New York City, 1972. ''It's not Western, it's Waylon,'' he says of his brand of country music.

Waylon is <u>the</u> man who invented chicken-pickin,' or "the stuttering guitar," as he calls it. As he once said, "I couldn't go pop with a mouthful of fire-crackers."

Nashville, Tennessee. Once one of the Crickets, a band led by Buddy Holly, Waylon Jennings narrowly avoided death when the Big Bopper took his seat on the small plane that crashed February 3, 1959, killing Holly, the Bopper, and Richie Valens.

Shaver, Kris Kristofferson, Kinky Friedman and Tompall Glaser. For they all did time walking that thin, white line that leads eventually to craziness.

When they got their first taste of money, they spent it like princes, and like princes they had contempt for moderation, often disdain for the law, and always a blazing desire to cut loose. And just when it seemed that those thin, midnight white lines were rolling so sweet and easy, they yanked themselves back from the edge—all except Hank, that is, who died the ignominious death of a modern-day outlaw, overdosing in the back seat of a chauffeured limousine.

Most of the Telecaster cowboys grew up in dire rural poverty: Hank on the flat, dry farmland around Georgiana, Alabama; Jerry Lee in the Louisiana swamps; Haggard in a trailer camp in Kern County, California; Cash in Dyess, Arkansas, where he watched his father coax a mule along under the hot sun, watched the blade of the gee-whiz catch in a root and bounce back on his father's shins. He remembered the flood of thirty-seven and the busted times. He learned that rural existence is hardly noble. "Anybody who thinks it is," said Cash, "ain't never been behind a mule when it backfired."

For Lewis, Haggard, Cash and Williams the sounds and the words of early country music, the songs of Jimmie Rodgers, the Carter Family, Bob Wills and Roy Acuff, were an almost mystical part of their makeup, a part of the soul from which there was no escape. They were later to escape from lives of rural poverty themselves—when each picked up the guitar, or in the case of Jerry Lee, sat down at a piano—but not from that raw gut feel for country music. It was as deeply ingrained as the farm dirt on their picking fingers.

It is these four—Lewis, Haggard, Cash and Williams (though there are many who might justifiably argue that Williams is the patron saint of the other three)—who could not be omitted from anybody's list of country-music outlaws. They are singled out for no reason other than that they have inspired countless imitators and are all recognized as having spawned "schools" of singing and musical styles.

Jerry Lee Lewis came out of Ferriday, Louisiana, in much the same way the others emerged from their home environments—

Merle Haggard. Nashville, Tennessee. He was in constant trouble as a young man—bogus checks, burglary, petty theft and finally armed robbery, which led to a three-year term in San Quentin. But this outlaw has since emerged as a writer and singer of such quality that his reputation has begun to rival that of even the great Hank Williams.

Jerry Lee Lewis. Memphis, Tennessee. He's called "the Killer" primarily because that's what he calls everybody else. He can drink more, roar louder, party longer, and sleep less than just about anybody, anywhere.

After three days without sleep, two days of drinking, and an all-night show in Vinton, Louisiana, Jerry Lee gets in the mood to cavort before the camera at 6 A.M. beside his private jet, which had just landed at the Memphis airport. From here, he drove off to his office to party. "I'm the greatest!" he says.

Jerry Lee behind his desk. One of the deepest of his many passions is his collection of old 78 r.p.m. records.

Johnny Paycheck. Nashville, Tennessee. Paycheck is a runaway kid from Greenfield, Ohio, who kept the wine and threw away the roses, then in the early seventies threw away the bottle and won the roses back.

quickly, and bringing much of the "country" with him. His hometown lay in the richest potpourri of music in America—the country, folk, and indigenous Cajun music of the white man, the blues and jazz of the black. Jerry Lee spent many nights in bars and clubs absorbing it all, and he had worked up his raw blend of arrogance and musical virtuosity on an old piano that his father had mortgaged the house to pay for.

He stormed his way into the SUN Records studios in Memphis, demanded an audition, and his "Whole Lotta Shakin' " was soon topping the national charts. The country boy had become a rock 'n' roller overnight, and he was the hottest property on the music scene, Elvis Presley excepted. His downfall (temporary, of course—most things with Jerry Lee are only temporary) was swift and sudden. He told the English press he had married his second cousin and came back to the United States to find that he was being made a whipping boy for a generation of "wayward" youth. He had been ready to take on the world, but the world was not ready for him. Jerry Lee was soon to be denounced as a work of the devil, outlawed at the tender age of twenty-three. He always swore that if he never had another rock hit, he would have one in country. Ten years later he did, and his country albums offer some of the finest "shit-kicking licks" ever laid down in a recording studio.

There are many stories about Jerry Lee Lewis, but my favorite is the tale of his receiving his first royalty check. It may have been embellished over the years, but it illustrates perfectly that when country boy Jerry Lee first stepped into the SUN studios he was about as sophisticated as five strands of barbed wire.

A few months after "Whole Lotta Shakin' " was released, Jerry Lee stopped by the SUN office to collect his first royalties —a whopping forty-two thousand dollars. He marched in on the owner, Sam Phillips, and demanded his money. Phillips reached for his checkbook, and Jerry Lee turned hostile. Assured that the check was as good as cash, he was finally persuaded to leave after promising to wreak all kinds of horrors on Sam Phillips's anatomy were the check to bounce. He crossed the street to a hotel that offered check-cashing facilities, where his worst suspicions were confirmed: The clerk did not have forty-two thousand dollars in cash readily available. Furious, Jerry

Tompall Glaser. Nashville, Tennessee. Formerly the black sheep of the Glaser Brothers, now solo. "Pinball and Jack Daniels are my vices," says the man who reputedly knows every pinball machine in Nashville and has seen many a sky turn gray before the dawn.

Billy Joe Shaver. Bryan, Texas. "His thoughts run deep and black," says
Tom T. Hall of the sensitive songwriter-performer who demands respect from
his audience or won't play. Wont just to disappear from anywhere, known as
a squirrel in Nashville, Billy Joe lost some fingers in a sawmill accident and
then learned to play the guitar.

Lee tore back to the SUN office. Phillips finally calmed him down by agreeing to call his bank manager and persuading him to open his bank, after hours, in order to make a special payment to Mr. Lewis.

Half an hour later Jerry Lee, still wearing jeans and a T-shirt, strolled into a Cadillac dealer's showroom. He smiled. The salesman frowned. "I want one of those," said the brash gum-popping kid.

"And what do you plan to use to pay for one of those?" asked the salesman.

"These," said Jerry Lee, and peeled off several one-thousand-dollar bills from his roll.

"Wild hair was all it was," Merle Haggard says now. "I was nailed on a burglary charge and wound up in San Quentin," where, as he says in his song "Mama Tried," "I turned twenty-one in prison doing life without parole." He was paroled, finally, after serving three years, returned to Bakersfield, put together a band, found himself a good ole boy manager, and eventually hit the road. He waited nearly seven years for fame.

Merle Haggard is much more than his patriotic hit song, "Okie From Muskogee." It is a shame, in a way, that "Okie" has tended to obscure the fact that he is one of the few genuine folk heroes in American music today. Haggard is no racist cracker spewing out Johnny Reb songs. As a songwriter he has managed to capture the life of the working man and portray it with an exceptional dignity. He is a restless, moody man, chain-smoking and intense—as real as the tattoo of a spiderweb on his back. He has been hailed as the "proletarian poet," and for a while he might have qualified, especially with his songs about boozing and unrequited love. But he is truly great when he turns to his own background for material, as in such songs as "Hungry Eyes," "Mama Tried," and "I Take a Lot of Pride in What I Am."

Most country outlaws have sown their wild oats. Haggard turned to crime, George Jones and Hank Williams to booze, Jerry Lee to a series of quick marriages and subsequent equally sudden divorces, Johnny Cash to pills.

Starting in 1961, Johnny Cash swallowed amphetamines by

the bottleful for eight years. When he first began taking them, he was performing 290 shows a year over a road circuit of 300,000 miles. In between he was making records. The strain compounded, and the drugs offered temporary relief.

But as Cash admits, the strain was only part of the reason. The other big problem was coping with success, and the easiest way to cope with success was to pretend it didn't happen. He hid behind practical jokes, outrageous acts of vandalism on the road and in hotels and, of course, the pills. "Maybe it was the miserable streak in me," he says today. "Maybe I was just afraid to face reality."

But folks identify with pain and suffering quicker than with anything else, and in the bars and factories and prisons, the fanatical following grew. Johnny Cash didn't need to build an image. He didn't even need the rhinestones and sequins that other country performers wore. A plain black frock coat and black pipe-stem trousers were enough. Johnny Cash didn't look too healthy during those hard, grinding years of the early sixties. The pain showed on his hollow face.

Cash represented the kind of rugged individualism so desperately sought after by the men in the Frigidaire plant, who saw it disappearing before their eyes. He was an impressive sight on stage, hunched over, chicken-picking an old Telecaster that looked like it had been purchased in a rummage sale. Years later, of course, came the TV show, and with it the charges that he had sold out. But by that time his legend was established and even American Oil commercials have done little to shake his vast following.

Hank Williams was, without question, the greatest country singer of them all. Although he died more than twenty years ago, his songs appear to have an endurance unparalleled in American popular music. His own reissued recordings still sell in staggering quantities, and songs like "Your Cheatin' Heart," "Jambalaya," "Hey, Good Lookin'" and "Take These Chains from My Heart" have been recorded by hundreds of artists in almost as many styles.

In the last twenty years, as the Williams legend has flourished, much is remembered about the last few years of his life, the private life that was so much in his public's eye. There is

David Allan Coe (with Mylon LeFevre). Bryan, Texas. David Allan first went to reform school at age nine and spent the next twenty years in and out of different prisons. His crimes ranged from car theft to possession of burglary tools to murder. He decided to become a professional musician when he realized that "I was as popular inside the penitentiary as Elvis Presley was in the street." David Allan has turned all his attention to writing and performing and has penned such tunes as "Will You Lay with Me (in a Field of Stone)," originally a wedding-ceremony song for his brother and eventually a hit for Tanya Tucker.

always the undercurrent of ugliness—drugs, liquor, insanity, overdose. There are those who glamorize him and those who despise him. He had a hard and sudden downfall when he was dismissed from the Grand Ole Opry because of his recurrent bouts with the bottle, although it was a decision that was to be expected, given the pristine image the Opry has always sought to maintain. Ironically, as soon as he was dead, it was the Opry officials, the very people who dismissed him, who worked hardest to build up his legend.

Hank's career began to come apart in the early fifties, as he reached the ripe old age of twenty-nine. But with all the publicity that attached itself to his decline, it is often forgotten that the millions who loved Hank and came to his concerts loved him because of, rather than in spite of, his problems. Like so many country singers, Hank's problem was the one he sang about: "The Lovesick Blues." Success could not allay the loneliness that gnawed at his insides. Nor could money. Money only bought him more booze to allow him to take his mind off the problem.

He sang the kinds of songs that are the wellspring of so much country music, songs about the inability of men and women to get along together. His own marriage was a turbulent one, and there is little doubt that his great songs—"Half as Much," "Why Don't You Love Me like You Used to Do," "I'm So Lonesome I Could Cry" and "Cold, Cold Heart"—were inspired by his own unhappy marital situation. It was this unhappiness that reached out to his audiences, to the grass roots. He communicated the kind of blues that people wanted to hear on the jukeboxes of the honky-tonk bars.

# 2

# The Kings and Queens of Country

Until the early fifties there were only kings. Country was an all-male preserve; no woman singer had ever achieved real stardom. Even Mother Maybelle Carter, of the original Carter Family, did not rank as a star in her own right. Then Johnny Wright met Muriel Deason in Mt. Juliet, Tennessee. Johnny was traveling with Jack Anglin, singing as a duo under the name Johnny and Jack, and Muriel up and married Johnny and joined the team as a gospel singer. She chose Kitty Wells as her pseudonym, and she remained known as Kitty Wells, gospel singer, until she recorded a song called "It Wasn't God Who Made Honky-Tonk Angels."

Most women's libbers have probably never heard of it, though it may well be the first women's lib song. It was an angry rebuff to a song by Hank Thompson, "The Wild Side of Life," a bitter little number that declared wicked, unfaithful women to be a creation of God. Kitty responded that "men were to blame," and several million country fans agreed. For many of the older fans, Kitty Wells is still the only queen of country music.

Long before Johnny Wright and Kitty Wells became a royal team (Johnny's partner, Jack, was killed in a car crash in 1964), there were solo male stars who were commonly known as kings of their profession. It is hard to define what it is that leads to the conferring of such a title (Hank Williams was never known as a king, nor were Johnny Cash or Merle Haggard). It may have something to do with sheer consistency, with length of service to country music or with simply being a fixture for years at the Grand Ole Opry, but whatever it is, Roy Acuff had it. If there is a king of the kings, Acuff is it, and no country fan would dispute this. He has played on the stage of the Opry for almost forty years; he was the Opry's first singing star, beginning a trend away from string bands; he is most closely identified with many of country music's most famous songs, including "Wabash Cannonball" and "The Great Speckled Bird"; he was the first living member to be elected to the Country Music Hall of Fame.

(Over) Roy Acuff. Nashville, Tennessee. Roy is the Opry's first singing star and the foremost King of Country Music.

Kitty Wells and Johnny Wright. Madison, Tennessee.

When Johnny Wright married Muriel Deason from Mt. Juliet, Tennessee, he renamed her after the Carter Family tune "I'm A-Goin' to Marry Kitty Wells." When she recorded "It Wasn't God Who Made Honky-Tonk Angels" in 1952, an angry rebuff to Hank Thompson's "The Wild Side of Life," she became the first female artist to have a number-one hit on the country charts. This song established her as the first Queen of Country Music.

Johnny Wright was the original Johnny of the Johnny and Jack Show, which Kitty eventually joined. The group ended when Jack Anglin was killed in a car accident in 1964.

Perhaps the greatest tribute to his international reputation came during World War II from reporter Ernie Pyle, who claimed in one of his reports from Okinawa that a Japanese battalion employed the battle cry: "To hell with President Roosevelt, to hell with Babe Ruth, to hell with Roy Acuff."

Roy Acuff was born in Maynardville, Tennessee, the son of a Baptist minister. His musical career began with a medicine show, fiddling and singing and dispensing a hair tonic that he still recommends. He tried his luck at baseball but was forced to cut short that career when he suffered a serious sunstroke. Acuff's early songs were largely middle-of-the-road classics like "Yes, Sir, That's My Baby," but in the mid-thirties he switched to the mournful, wailing style of singing that was more natural to his Smoky Mountain heritage. It was the many lonesome-sounding melodies recorded in this style that made him famous.

Like most kings, Acuff tends to be conservative and traditional. He is a staunch Republican who makes no secret of the fact that he is a firm believer in traditional American values and an ardent foe of anybody who disagrees with those values. "I don't respect hippies," he has said, "because I don't think that they have any respect for anything." But he has a great respect and affinity for country people and country ways. His one serious fling with politics was in the 1940s, when the then governor of Tennessee pronounced hillbilly music "disgraceful." Acuff ran against him, but in spite of his obvious identification with the virtues of God, home and mother, he didn't make it to the governor's mansion.

These days Acuff is largely content to mind his various business enterprises, such as the Acuff-Rose Publishing Company, which he started in 1942 with songwriter Fred Rose, and to sing at the Opry on Friday and Saturday nights. He still wears his crown but not as exclusively as he did at one time. When the popular acclaim for another star caused him to have to share it, it was with a singer whose style, though very different from Acuff's, was as deeply rooted in country tradition.

This singer was George Jones, who grew up in Saratoga, Texas, far from cattle country, in the heart of an area where rural life was giving way to urban. Nonetheless, the radio and the local honky-tonks still poured out a stream of hillbilly music, and Jones grew up listening to the likes of Acuff and Ernest

Tammy Wynette and George Jones (with daughter Georgette). Nashville, Tennessee. When Wynette Pugh married George Jones, the then Crown Prince of Country Music, she fulfilled her lifelong dream. Little did she realize that a few years, Billy Sherrill, and numerous number-one hits later she would be a queen in her own right.

Before their divorce, this king and queen lived in a $500,000 modern mansion just outside Nashville. The mansion's wrought-iron gates are made up of the notes of "Stand by Your Man." Amid rumors of on-again off-again divorce and reconciliation, Tammy and George's romance was the real-life stuff of which country songs are made. Ironically, Tammy's two biggest songs were "D*I*V*O*R*C*E" and "Stand by Your Man."

Tubb, whose styles are still very much reflected in his own brand of phrasing. His greatest success came in the early sixties, when he recorded many of his best songs ("Don't Stop the Music" and "Just One More" among others) and when the first wave of honky-tonk resurgence took hold with the record-buying public.

But there is an ironic twist to the George Jones story. Although he is still a firm favorite with hard-core country fans and lovers of the traditional style of singing, his reign as a king was a comparatively short one. New performers like Cash and Haggard emerged in the sixties to steal the spotlight, and although Jones continued to record many fine albums, he never reproduced that commercial formula that had given him so many chart-topping successes. One of George Jones's fans in his chart-topping days was a teenage girl from Tupelo, Mississippi, named Wynette Pugh. When she left school, she became a hairdresser but left that profession to try her luck in Nashville's Music Row, just one of many hometown honeys looking for the big break.

She was discovered by Billy Sherrill, Nashville's producer extraordinaire, and when she hit the big time, she hit it bigger than any female country singer to emerge in the sixties. When the producers of Five Easy Pieces wanted to epitomize country music in their film, they chose Tammy Wynette's recording of "Stand By Your Man." Tammy married her childhood hero, George Jones, and until their recent divorce they took over from Kitty Wells and Johnny Wright as the new, undisputed King and Queen of Country Music. It was true that Tammy was far and away the bigger breadwinner, but this was of little importance to the former couple's fans. George has a track record of writing and singing hit songs which few can equal, so even if it is Tammy who these days occupies most of the limelight, they are regarded with equal awe by their legion of admirers.

Male-female vocal duos have found a solid niche in country music. Aside from a husband-and-wife team like George and Tammy, there are many others whose association is purely professional. Loretta Lynn has teamed up with Conway Twitty to record some excellent country material; Porter Wagoner hired Dolly Parton to fill a vacant female solo spot on his syndicated TV show and ended up realizing that his own singing voice could be greatly enhanced by the addition of Dolly's fine Ten-

Porter Wagoner. Nashville, Tennessee.

A farm boy who spent his childhood pretending he was a singing star, Porter Wagoner grew up to be one. His first chance came when his boss, a butcher, asked him to do a fifteen-minute radio show from his shop, singing and advertising the meat specials of the day. Today his syndicated TV show makes him one of the most familiar faces in country.

Dolly Parton. Nashville, Tennessee. Replacing singer Norma Jean, Dolly became Porter's queen. She's five foot two inches of bingles, bangles and baubles, but below those towering mounds of blonde hair is a songwriting brain that proves once and for all that blondes are not necessarily dumb. Dolly has now left the Porter Wagoner Show and is solo.

nessee twang. Buck Owens teamed up with Susan Raye to record albums, and for many years Bill Anderson and Jan Howard were part of the same road show.

Country fans, like all fans, love to dwell on the details of their heroes' personal lives, but the difference between the country fan and, say, the movie star devotee is that the former demands that the star's image be as close to pristine as is possible. By and large, fans refused to believe that Tammy Wynette and George Jones had stumbled on troubled times, even after Tammy filed divorce papers in 1973 (subsequently retracted) and again in 1974 and alleged that George was hitting the bottle too hard. How could they believe this after the message of "Stand By Your Man"? And it was no accident, certainly, that once the difficulties were patched up this last time, George and Tammy's next duet was a simple, positive song called "We're Gonna Hold On." It was almost a reaffirmation of their fans' former faith.

Country fans will do anything for their heroes except leave them alone. There is constant scrutiny of the stars' lives. Every detail of their existence is digested, every iota of gossip absorbed. This isn't an ordinary record-buying public; country fans look to their stars for example. Even if the stars' wealth and stature are poles apart from those of their audience, they share the same roots, and there is constant identification.

The stars are well aware that to be part of a male-female duo enhances fan appeal. It draws added attention, gives a big fix of the very insulin of the entertainment business: glamour. It almost doesn't matter if the relationship is purely professional. It is the image on stage that counts—simply looking like a couple. God knows how many countless fans are unable to distinguish Porter Wagoner and Dolly Parton as other than man and wife.

Dolly Parton has now left the Porter Wagoner Show, but she is still very much a queen in her own right. She is an extremely beautiful woman whose projected country innocence seems to enable other less well endowed women to excuse all that flamboyance that is Dolly's style—towering mounds of blonde hair, curves reminiscent of Monroe, jewelry galore, and lots of makeup. "It's not that I'm trying to show off," she says. "It's just that when I was little in Sevierville, Tennessee, I never had anything at all, and when I would see someone dressed up real fancy, that would impress me no end. I'm just like any other women with five wigs; I just like to wear this stuff all at once."

Loretta Lynn (with Mooney). Hurricane Mills, Tennessee. Loretta is country music's most renowned rags-to-riches story. She grew up in dire poverty in Butcher Hollow, Kentucky, married Mooney when she was thirteen, had four children by the time she was eighteen, and became a grandmother at twenty-

eight. Now the couple owns an entire town in Tennessee, plus a large ranch and antebellum manor house, and runs a rodeo as well as a number of music-publishing companies. Yet Loretta is still the quintessential country girl.

Aside from all that "stuff," the range, subject matter and musical form of the songs she writes is amazing. Within the canon of country music, she has tried everything, and when the resources of country have seemed too limited, she has borrowed from elsewhere—from folk, rock or jazz. She also shares a great sense of community with her audience and manages to do so with subject matter that is decidedly off-color—about suicide, adultery, betrayal, incestuous desire. She is a dedicated musician whose career leaves little time for anything else. When she's on the road, she will sometimes stay up late writing songs, often dictating lyrics to a secretary. Unlike many other female country singers, she makes no claims to being domestic, and she frankly admits that she and her husband lead very independent lives.

Her voice is thin, almost shrill, but it is a voice very much prized among female country singers, and it has a great deal in common with that of another prominent lady in country music, Loretta Lynn. Loretta Lynn teams up for duo spots with Conway Twitty, but like Dolly she is very much her own woman, a solo star in her own right. Like Dolly she also grew up in the mountains, in Butcher Hollow, Kentucky, where she was married when she was thirteen years old. Her husband, Mooney, took her off to the Northwest, where she got her start singing while he busted broncs. By the time she was eighteen, she had four kids, and although she is a grandmother today, she still looks young enough to have another four. She and her husband now run a business empire that includes music-publishing companies, a chain of western-wear stores, the largest private rodeo in the world and a whole town in Tennessee. It is a success story that is surpassed by no one in the world of country music.

Today Loretta Lynn still hits the country charts' top position consistently. When she's not on the road, working the incredible number of dates that she does, she is either in the recording studio or looking after her business interests. Yet she still cannot read well enough to pass the written test for her driver's license. She is, in other words, a natural, and this naturalness allows her at any time to revert to being the quintessential country girl whose simplicity is the cornerstone of her appeal to her millions of fans.

Conway Twitty. Oklahoma City, Oklahoma. Born Harold Jenkins, he acquired his stage name by picking places off a map: Conway, Arkansas, and Twitty, Texas. After a long, successful career in rock music, with hits like "It's Only Make Believe," Conway returned to his roots. His duet records with Loretta Lynn are among the most popular in country music.

Buck Owens. Bakersfield, California. Owens runs a country-music empire that is so successful and significant that Bakersfield, where his headquarters are located, has been dubbed Buckersfield and Little Nashville.

Susan Raye. Bakersfield, California. Susan was discovered by Buck Owens
in Portland, Oregon, when she was still a teenager. He waited for her to grow
up, then invited her to join his Owens All-American Show. Now she lives in
Bakersfield as part of the Owens "family" and frequently teams up with him
for duets.

There is, of course, one other couple that will still pack a hall with ten-thousand-plus admirers, whether it be in Portland, Oregon, or Portland, Maine. Johnny Cash and June Carter's recording of "Jackson" is still probably the finest country duet ever recorded. The difference with Carter and Cash is that they don't bill themselves as a duo so much as a family. Their road shows include Mother Maybelle; her daughters, June, Helen and Anita; Carl Perkins and until recently the Statler Brothers quartet. This is more than a family; it's a royal family. And on the road it's a sight to see. And perhaps the most amazing figure in the group is Mother Maybelle, the quiet elderly lady who stands in the background just picking the autoharp because she can't play a guitar as often these days because of her arthritis. She plays a style of guitar that she herself developed which has become the basic picking style for a million country tunes. She is a modest lady. And she is a trouper. When everyone else is getting run-down and bad tempered, she will just quietly keep on going. She will load a dozen bags into the bus before anyone else has noticed.

If you get her in a quiet moment and ask her about her early years, she may tell you about her recordings with Jimmie Rodgers, when she and the Carter Family recorded with him in Texas in 1932. She will tell you how sick he was, how he couldn't get up from the cot because the T.B. had already laid him low. And with an almost girlish smile, she might add: "They think that's him playing guitar on that album, but it isn't, you know; it's me."

She is the true first lady of country music.

# 3
# The New Wave

Nobody can give you an exact date when it started. At first nobody was really sure if it was "country." All anyone can say for certain is that in those last few years of the giddy sixties a steady stream of new faces and new sounds emerged from the Nashville recording studios and began displacing the established stars in the country charts. These new singers changed the face of country music forever. They bit deep and hard into the sales of three-chord staple lame love songs that for so long had dominated the country charts. The new lyrics were as honest and raw and double-edged as anything the Rolling Stones had released, and the song structures were sometimes as complex as the most elaborate rock production.

The media confused everything by calling it the Nashville Sound, an idiotic hype that implied a uniformity to what was essentially a new diversity. The term Nashville Sound was as ridiculous a notion as the idea that country was strong again because conservatism had been reestablished under Richard Nixon, the kind of Life magazine philosophy that could conveniently ignore the fact that rock 'n' roll had blossomed under the Eisenhower administration. But the term stuck, and for a while recording in Nashville became chic, especially for a few rock musicians, who saw their Nashville recording sessions as a kind of musical Easy Rider adventure.

But the seeds of the New Wave had been sown long before the new country music appeared on the charts. As a recording center Nashville had been growing steadily ever since the fifties, when country refused to die under the first onslaught of rock 'n' roll. Its studios had lured a talented range of instrumentalists, sidemen or "pickers," as they are known in Nashville, who had found steady employ as backup musicians to the country stars. Over the years they had grown accustomed to working together. They'd even designed a new musical code

(Over) Kris Kristofferson. Nashville, Tennessee. A former West Pointer, Rhodes scholar, helicopter pilot and general cleanup man at Columbia Studios in Nashville for fifty-eight dollars a week, Kristofferson scored points with hippies and God-fearing folk, respectively by writing such songs as "Me and Bobby McGee" and "Why Me, Lord?" He led the New Wave of musicians who changed the face of country music.

based on numbers instead of the standard musical notation. They were very quick at assimilating parts, thus reducing the extraordinarily high costs of recording time, and they were tight and consistent. They were also bored stiff, their talents vastly underutilized by the inevitable restrictions imposed by the traditional three-chord country songs. But they weren't about to rock any boats; steady, high-paying work is a very desirable commodity for backup musicians, so for the most part they were prepared to sit tight and satisfy the simple demands of the country producers, who simply cranked out the same repetitive diet.

It might have been this way still if Bob Dylan hadn't paid the town a visit in 1966 and 1967 and used several Nashville sidemen to record his Blonde on Blonde album. Dylan hired harmonica player Charlie McCoy, guitarist Wayne Moss, Kenny Buttrey on drums, Hargus Robbins on piano and Henry Strzelecki on bass. For most of them it was the first time they'd ever heard anything like this. The excitement generated by the session spread round Nashville like a brushfire. "The pickers didn't know what to make of lines like 'forty pounds of headlights stapled to his chest,'" said one sideman. "It was a meeting of two wholly different musical worlds."

And the pickers had to respect Dylan. He was "Dylan" after all, and hadn't no less than Johnny Cash endorsed him and later even recorded with him? Suddenly the walls between rock and country began to crumble. Overnight it seemed as if everybody was aware of new possibilities. The steel gates of the world of country had creaked slightly open and some new influences had peeked inside. Then another formerly deaf-mute segment of Nashville's music scene began to make rumbles: the songwriters, at least the younger ones newly arrived in town, decided that they had had enough of country music's spin dryer view of the world. New lyrics began to confront real issues, doing what country had neglected to do for a long time—tell it like it is—and above all facing up to that most touchy of subjects, sex. It was a musical equivalent of all that pubic hair suddenly appearing on the Playboy models.

Of course the New Wave stirred some protest. Charges were made that this burgeoning of new talent and fresh ideas was pushing country too far uptown. It was an unfair charge; in

Tanya Tucker. Little Rock, Arkansas. The superstarlette of country music, Tanya sings sexy songs usually reserved for women older than she. Here she turns sixteen.

Johnny Rodriguez. Brentwood, Tennessee. The new sex symbol of country music—watch those Southern ladies turn out to see him—this Mexican-American country star was playing guitar in a Texas jail to pass the time he was serving for goat-rustling, and so impressed the state trooper who arrested him, that he drove him to Brackettville where he got him a job at Alamo Village, a popular tourist spot. There Tom T. Hall and Bobby Bare discovered him. After working as a guitarist in Tom T. Hall's band, he had a hit in his first solo year with "Pass Me By."

Sammi Smith. Bryan, Texas. A very promising singing star, Sammi has had one big hit so far, but there'll be others to come. She's usually found hanging out with the rest of the outlaws who revolve around the Willie Nelson-Waylon Jennings axis.

fact, it was the opposite of the truth. For the most part the move uptown was made by the already established country performers—Ray Price, Glen Campbell, Bill Anderson, Sonny James and many others—who saw their own brand of country as outdated and forsook their rhinestones and cowboy boots for dress shoes and tuxedos. They played down their country images and hard country songs, and they took to the suburban side roads as all-round entertainers. The newcomers, on the other hand—singers such as Tanya Tucker, Johnny Rodriguez and Jimmy Buffett—made no attempt to conceal their country origins and styles of singing.

The New Wave showed itself perfectly capable of accommodating as "country" both long-haired intellectuals and crew-cut good ole boys. As examples of these respective categories, it offered up Kris Kristofferson and Tom T. Hall, both of whom wrote songs with a new realism and honesty, dealing with sensitive subjects.

Kristofferson was a Rhodes scholar and a West Point dropout who worked at a series of menial jobs in Nashville until his songs began to find favor in the right places. He found a powerful patron in Johnny Cash, who recorded some of his best material, such as "Sunday Morning Coming Down," and whose endorsement was sufficient to make sure that the eyebrows raised over his long hair and hippie guise went no further than being raised eyebrows. The overwhelming attitude toward him among hard-core country fans was "Damn it, I don't much go for his looks, but he sure can write one helluva fine song."

Tom T. Hall, on the other hand, moved in the reverse direction. A lot of Hall's current campus admirers are unaware that in 1964 he was writing pro-war ditties, such as "Hello, Vietnam." Hall underwent what at one time was known as a greening. He is a good ole boy from Kentucky who saw that attitudes were changing and whose songs are full of the ironies caused by those changes. He has never been afraid to acknowledge, sympathetically, the weaknesses of human nature in his lyrics, with songs such as "Harper Valley P.T.A.," the story of a wayward lady who ticks off a P.T.A. meeting for its hypocrisy, and "Margie's at the Lincoln Park Inn," the story of a man whose wife is "bakin' cookies" and who just happens to be out of cigarettes, and Margie just happens to be at the Inn he goes to.

66

Anne Murray. Lake Tahoe, Nevada. "The singing sweetheart of Canada" plays down her peaches-and-cream wholesome-girl-next-door looks, guzzles beer in public and loves to shock her audiences. Liberated? You bet.

Jimmy Buffett. Bryan, Texas. The up-and-coming darling of the intellectual country fans, Jimmy is a prime example of the youth movement coming to terms with country music. His first album was called "A White Sports Coat and a Pink Crustacean."

Ronnie Milsap. Nashville, Tennessee. A brilliant blind pianist and singer who became a big draw in Nashville when he performed every night on the roof of the King of the Road, Ronnie is a ham-radio operator and collects tapes of old radio shows when he's not busy with his first love, creating music. →

Kristofferson and Hall were pioneers of the New Wave, and their popular acceptance paved the way for a deluge of new young performers. If Kristofferson had not eroded the last remnants of prejudice in the Opry audience, it would have been unthinkable for the likes of Kinky Friedman and his Texas Jewboys to have been on that sacred stage five years later. Likewise, if Hall had not made risqué lyrics acceptable, Freddy Weller would never have gotten away with autobiographical songs about first-time motel-room conquests.

And with the arrival of all this new blood, performers like Jimmy Buffett, Tanya Tucker, Johnny Rodriguez, Billy Joe Shaver, Don Williams, Anne Murray, the Nitty Gritty Dirt Band, David Allan Coe, Doug Kershaw, Kinky Friedman and many more, a change occurred in the whole structure. The Opry was no longer the looming monolith it had been previously, the country musician's guardian, moral and otherwise, the focal point of country stars' lives, where membership was almost obligatory if you wanted to be known by the label "country." Many new singers declined to join, remaining content with a mere guest appearance. They were making so much money on tour that to be rigidly confined by the Opry's obligatory number of appearances (at unbelievably low wages) would have been a handicap to their careers. They just didn't need the Opry anymore. Even singers who had been members for a while, such as Tom T. Hall, decided that an amicable parting of the ways was worthwhile.

The New Wave also brought a spate of new record companies into the country-music business—or at least record companies that until the late sixties and early seventies had been successful with rock but had omitted country artists from their rosters. As the boundaries blurred and more and more young, bestselling singers proved to be unabashed by the label "country," these companies decided it was financially worth their while to have a place of business and recording facilities in Nashville. They brought with them a new style, a new urgency and a new competitiveness to the business. They saw that country was not just a temporary fad but a musical form to which many new performers would be attracted now that younger musicians had broken through its isolationism and that the strict boundaries that Tin Pan Alley had imposed on the world of music had been broken down.

Freddy Weller. Nashville, Tennessee. For years a member of Paul Revere and the Raiders, Freddy has lately returned to country, where he began. He writes of love and lust in such songs as "Perfect Stranger" and "Sexy Lady." Here he attracts a fan as he relaxes in Tootsie's Orchid Lounge, a legendary watering hole near the Ryman Auditorium.

Doug Sahm and Spanky McFarland. Bryan, Texas. Part of the rock/country bridge, they've both been a big influence on the Nashville underground.

Alex Harvey. Bryan, Texas. Harvey co-wrote "Delta Dawn," one of country's recent classics, with Larry Collins. He's still an underground star in Nashville, but just wait!

But more important than the structure of the whole business and the arrival of new record companies in Nashville was the assault of new sounds on the airwaves. No longer was there any legitimacy to the criticism that a lot of country music sounded the same. The new voices paid no deference to the communal country mold, the philosophy that demanded that your phrasing be modeled after a "true great," such as Hank Williams or George Jones. Which is not to say that there was no evidence of the influence of the greats in the styles of the new-comers; it was just that they seemed to arrive with their individual styles already developed, making them instantly recognizable at a second hearing.

Take the youngest of the new stars, for example: Sixteen-year-old Tanya Tucker's voice hits you like an Arizona sandstorm. Its rushing nasal quality can send shivers down your spine. In personal appearances it is hard to believe that this seasoned sound emanates from the throat and lungs of a teenage girl. And she certainly didn't sing "little girl" songs; her producer at Columbia Records, Billy Sherrill, saw to that. One of her recordings, written by David Allan Coe, another New Wave personality, was called "Will You Lay with Me (in a Field of Stone)."

When Tanya started touring, she was paired with a twenty-one-year-old Mexican-American singer named Johnny Rodriguez. He was a protege of Tom T. Hall's, discovered near San Antonio, playing guitar for a living at a local tourist spot, Alamo Village. Hall brought him to Nashville and set him in front of Mercury Records' executives, who were smart enough to know a hot property when they saw one. Within months Rodriguez was an established solo performer who set Southern females screaming in a way that hadn't been seen since Presley. His voice is uniquely country, an exquisite, soulful whine, but his dark-haired youthful good looks counted for something, too. With Tanya pulling in the cowboys and Rodriguez charming the ladies, the two were soon packing stadiums throughout the South and West.

But Tanya Tucker and Johnny Rodriguez were clean-cut kids compared to some newcomers on the country scene. The New Wave brought with it new outlaws who didn't give a damn about traditional appearances or whether their songs were considered country or not. They found favor without asking for it.

← Charley Pride. Nashville, Tennessee. Country music's first black star, Charley Pride was voted Entertainer of the Year by the Country Music Association in 1972.

Kinky Friedman at his ranch, Rio Duckworth, in Texas.

I once watched Billy Joe Shaver pacing backstage at the Dripping Springs Festival in Texas. It was one of his first public appearances, certainly the largest crowd he'd ever sung in front of, and he was downing cans of Lone Star and Jax beer so fast you'd have thought someone was about to revive Prohibition. Finally he grabbed his guitar and dragged himself onto the stage. "This song's about a colored chick," he blurted. There was a stunned silence, broken by a few catcalls and one loud whoopee. Then Billy Joe launched into "Black Rose," telling how "the devil made me do it first time / The second time I done it on my own." He walked offstage to one of the greatest ovations I have ever heard for a country singer.

The same went for Kinky Friedman when he first played the Opry. He had toned down his act slightly, but he was still wearing his outrageous American-flag-and-Star-of-David–decorated outfit. He left the stage to huge applause and was collared by one of the Opry's stodgier old-time officials. "You know, Kinky," the official told him, "I know a good country song when I hears one, and that song of yours, 'Sold American,' that's a damn fine country song."

Friedman's repertoire is nonetheless pretty far into left field even for the New Wave. It includes a song about Charles Whitman, who shot thirteen people dead from the University of Texas Tower in Austin, an anti–women's lib number called "Get Your Biscuits in the Oven and Your Buns in the Bed" and an anti-redneck song called "We Reserve The Right to Refuse Service to You." For the most part his singing engagements are carefully selected, and he avoids venues that may result in his suffering grievous bodily harm. But Friedman is the exception, and other hard-hitting lyricists such as Jimmy Buffett and John Prine have no such problem. Prine is a Vietnam vet who was the first country singer to look the veteran's big problem squarely in the eye: "There's a hole in Daddy's arm where all the money goes." Buffett, like Tom T. Hall, picks up everyday problems and confronts them sympathetically, as in "Peanut Butter Conspiracy," a song about the art of pinching food from supermarkets.

The New Wave performers did not have to maintain the kind of fairy-tale image that the older stars did. Tales of excess about Doug Kershaw, the wild man from Louisiana, crazed Cajun fiddler supreme, only boosted his popularity with his fans.

Don Williams. Nashville, Tennessee. Formerly a pop singer, Don, with his pure, rich country voice, is making Nashville listen. So far he's recorded three first-rate solo albums.

Willie Nelson. Bryan, Texas. He paved the way for the new breed of country songwriter. The most famous representative of the "Austin Sound," Willie organizes a country-music festival in Texas each summer.

Leon Russell. New York City, 1970.

Leon Russell with Willie Nelson. Leon performs and records country music under the alias Hank Wilson. Not that his alias is any secret.

Asleep at the Wheel. Nashville, Tennessee. This group from San Francisco plays terrific country swing.

Larry Gatlin. Antioch, Tennessee. A protege of Cash and Kristofferson, Gatlin
has impressed the songwriting establishment with such songs as "Penny Annie."

Tracy Nelson. Nashville, Tennessee, 1970. Tracy is very much part of the Nashville underground but as much at home with the blues as with country.

Mac Davis. Harpeth Hills, Tennessee.

Lloyd Green. Nashville, Tennessee. Green is Nashville's "A Team" pedal steel guitarist.

Red Lane. Bryan, Texas. Lane looks like a "good ole country hoss" yet is considered one of the finest new poets in country.

Michael Murphy. Bryan, Texas. One of the bright stars of the "Austin Sound,"
Murphy finally hit it big with "Wildfire."

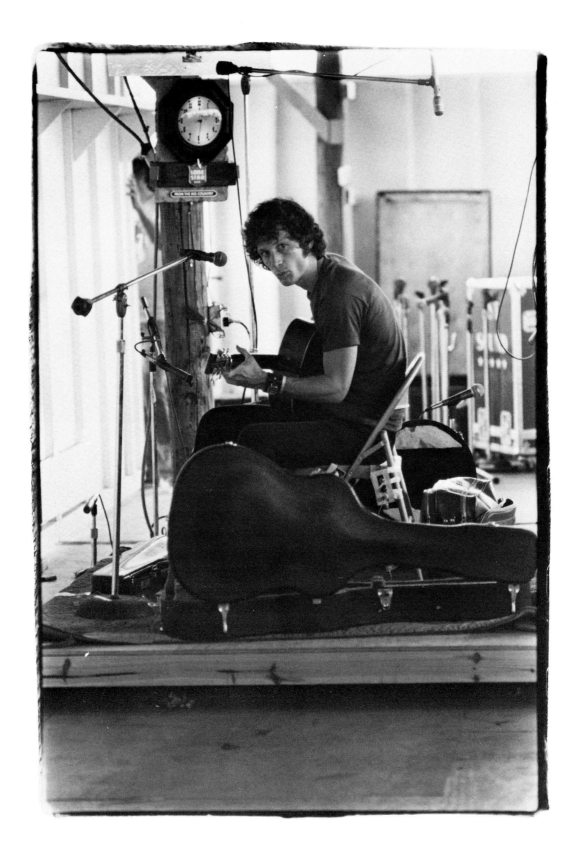

John Hartford. Bryan, Texas. The writer of the country classic "Gentle on My Mind" tunes his guitar before a performance.

Vassar Clements. Equally at home with country and rock music, Clements often performs with the Allman Brothers.

Guy Clark. Bryan, Texas.

Mickey Newbury. Old Hickory Lake, Tennessee. A reticent performer, Newbury is considered one of the most important songwriters in Nashville. "Frisco
Mabel Joy" and "She Even Woke Me Up to Say Good-bye" are his.

He suffered none of the public whippings that Jerry Lee Lewis was subjected to in the fifties when tales of his escapades filtered back to his fans via the press. Jerry Lee had to wait until the times were right for country fans to recognize what a superb performer he was. Neither did the New Wave women, Anne Murray and Sammi Smith, have to project the butter-wouldn't-melt-in-their-mouths image that the previous women stars of country music had been saddled with. Anne Murray didn't care less about it being reported that she drank beer while being interviewed.

In all fairness it must be said that many of the older country performers lent their endorsement to the new entertainers, and this in itself was a way of making them quickly acceptable to the more conservative faction of fans. The Nitty Gritty Dirt Band, a group of city boys who play country music as authentic as that of any of the old-timers, received a tremendous boost when Roy Acuff, Mother Maybelle Carter, Doc Watson and Earl Scruggs agreed to guest on a triple-album recording of the Dirt Band's called "Will the Circle Be Unbroken?" It is as fine a recording of old styles blended with new as any available. Roy Acuff's one regret about the session: "I niver did git to see their faces."

There is one other singer who deserves more than passing mention here because he more than any other was a first for country music: Charley Pride, country's first black singer. Pride grew up in Texas, listened to the sounds of country music, ignored the questions of friends who asked, "Why are you listening to their music?" and was discovered by a canny manager who believed the time was right for a black singer in country. Pride made some tapes that were played for R.C.A. record executives. "Nice voice, fine country voice," said one listener. "Who is he?" The manager produced a photo. "You're kidding!" exclaimed the executive.

But manager Jack Johnson was not kidding, and Charley Pride was signed with R.C.A. In the last ten years his albums have outsold any other contemporary country performer's. He was voted Entertainer of the Year by the Country Music Association in 1972 and was one of the first country entertainers to be admitted to the hallowed halls of the Las Vegas Hilton. His voice is universally acknowledged to be one of the finest country voices around today.

Barbara Fairchild. Nashville, Tennessee. Her first songs on Columbia soared to the top of the charts, and she was quickly being compared with such stars as Loretta Lynn.

Jack Johnson is still amazed at the reception Charley Pride receives throughout white rural America. "I've seen big burly truckers with their arms draped round his shoulders, posing with him for pictures. If you told some of these guys they was going to have a colored guy as a co-driver, they'd go nuts. But then you gotta realize Charley is special. He ain't no phony. He <u>loves</u> country music. He <u>is</u> country. He <u>feels</u> it."

A reporter I know once heard an upstate New York farmer ask Hank Williams, "Hank, where'd you learn to sing the blues?"

"I learned everthin' about singin' from a fine old Mississippi nigra I used to foller aroun' when I was a kid," Hank replied.

A few years ago the reporter was backstage at a Charley Pride concert in New Jersey.

"Hey, Charley," someone asked. "Where'd you learn to sing the 'Lovesick Blues' like that?"

"From listening to Hank Williams," Charley answered. "Where else?"

# 4
# Plastic Rose Country Dream Living

The country musician's life loses a lot of its glamour when he or she hits the road. In spite of the luxury of the $100,000 custom-made Silver Eagle buses, those long hours between engagements are monotonous and grueling. Recognition at every roadside stop can be a strain; diets revert to quick meals and Alka Seltzers; autograph hunters and well-wishers disrupt any remnants of privacy; every new concert venue has a sound system with a mind of its own. But when you're hot, you're hot, and you'd better hit every small town from New Mexico to New Hampshire (and there are quite a few) if you want those records to sell.

Fortunately, the modern country musician, unlike the balladeer of yore, has something to come home to, and these days that something is likely to be fairly substantial—often a few hundred acres and a property with enough rooms to rival San Simeon. If you wonder why there aren't so many country songs written today about hopping freights, meeting hobos and bumming dimes, it's because a fair quotient of today's country singers have never hopped a freight, met a hobo or bummed a dime in their lives. This wasn't the case only a few years ago. Such singers as Hank Snow knew all about movin' on, and many similar old timers' songs were simply a reflection of their life-styles. But while many of today's performers might sing the songs of Jimmie Rodgers, celebrating the life of a railroad bum, their own life-styles consist of wearing golf slax to the office as well as to the pro-celebrity tournament and spending Sunday afternoons tending to manicured lawns in the suburbs. There's a certain irony attached to being well-fed defenders of poor man's music.

"Nashville is a groovy little town," Tom T. Hall sang back in the sixties. Indeed it was, and it still is as one makes one's way through the songwriter world of bars along West End, listening to the hopefuls recite their latest lyrics, dropping in at any of several small clubs where you can still hear high-priced talent pop off a few licks for friends in an ambience as casual

(Over) Loretta Lynn in her garden.

98

Dottie West. Nashville, Tennessee. Her career took an upward turn with the help of the Coca-Cola Company and her hit from the Coke commercial, "Country Sunshine."

Jeanne Pruett. Nashville, Tennessee. After years of obscurity working for Marty Robbins and raising two kids now in their teens, Jeanne Pruett finally hit it big with "Satin Sheets." She won't admit to using them.

Barbara Mandrell. Nashville, Tennessee. Here Barbara is in her dressing room before a Hee Haw taping. Barbara does not allow her musicians to drink or smoke on stage or even wear blue jeans when they travel. "My rules make it hard to get good musicians," she admits.

and down home as any you're likely to find these days. But Nashville is also a booming business town where one of the most successful businesses is music, and on Music Row you will see some of the fallout of this success, enormous hydramatically suspended monster cars cruising in front of the sumptuous record company offices or snuggling into their reserved parking spaces. For a certain life-style has evolved among the entertainers, P.R. men, A & R men, producers and publicists which is about as country as Hollywood Hills.

Success among the country-music community has produced some strange sights.

"It's not surprising," says one member of the community whose own house is fitted out in what could be called, by Good Housekeeping standards, good taste. "Most of the people who made it big in this business grew up in what was close to extreme poverty. In their early lives they were denied what many of us would have considered the most basic living requirements. When some of the country stars were kids, the best they could expect for Christmas was a few pieces of fruit and lots of wrapping paper. No wonder when somebody gave 'em an old beat-up guitar they treated it like gold and learned to play it."

Childhood poverty and subsequent (and often sudden) wealth enhanced the desire to consume, and the consumption often involved material features that could only be described as striking in their ostentatiousness. It is not for nothing that Nashville has been called the plastic-rose capital of the world. There are artifacts here on people's front lawns and hanging from office walls which would amaze even visitors from Coral Gables. There's a certain competitiveness attached to the consumption, sending the whole snowball hurtling forward in what seems like a mad scramble to assemble all the world's available kitsch in one town. Everybody knows that even if Webb Pierce were forgotten for the songs he sang, he would be remembered for being the first country star to install a guitar-shaped swimming pool.

And in Nashville your success is often measured by how much you're prepared to flaunt it. Every country star will admit to the public pressure to own a brand-new Cadillac. It's almost expected. If you don't, it's assumed that maybe your records

Bobby Bare (and his family). Hendersonville, Tennessee. The Bares romp in the lake behind the house that "we first saw eight years ago but couldn't nearly afford." Recently Bobby recorded an entire album of songs written by Shel Silverstein.

Lynn Anderson (and daughter Lisa). Brentwood, Tennessee. Her life is every bit a "Rose Garden." She's married to hit record producer Glenn Sutton and spends much of her spare time with her championship horses.

aren't doing so well, and nobody in this business wants to let assumptions like that get around. So the result is a proliferation of Cadillacs with all kinds of special options, a car that must be traded for a new model as often as the prevailing taste of the community dictates.

It is often said that Nashville imitates Hollywood, that the country musician's real aspiration is to play in Vegas and live in Beverly Hills. There are a certain number of country musicians abandoning Nashville to do just this. But even among those who remain, the Hollywood syndrome has been adopted wholesale. This author recently made a trip from Hollywood (where turquoise jewelry was the rage) to find that it was also the rage among the country stars, and in the United States the two communities probably rank one and two when it comes to crystal chandeliers and antiqued furniture labeled Birmingham, England.

The parallels with Beverly Hills extend further. From downtown Nashville you can take a bus tour, just as you can in Hollywood, which takes you past the homes of the stars. Many of these homes still strive for a pretense of country living. Stars will talk about their ranches, which only derive this name from the name the realtor gave them—ranchettes—and many of these properties now lie in areas that in all honesty could only be called suburban. Some parts of Queens in New York City are more rural. Fishing on the exquisite lakes an hour away from the city is still an entirely big deal among the country music community, but these days you can't underestimate the importance of golf.

The life-style in Nashville has evolved in the same way the music has evolved; the prevailing drift has been uptown. Once the country-music community, with its rural ways and habits, was almost an embarrassment to the city fathers, those worthies of pursuits more respectable than "hillbilly music," as they disdainfully branded it; but these days the country stars are on a par with the Southern gentry. Not that the gulf has broken down entirely. There's still only one corporation in Nashville which pays any real attention to country music. This is the National Life and Accident Insurance Company, owners of Opryland and WSM, the radio station that broadcasts the Grand Ole Opry.

Sonny James. Old Hickory Lake, Tennessee. "The Country Gentleman" first made it big in pop with "Young Love" but never gave up his Nashville base. He spends his spare time on Center Hill Lake. When he's lucky, he comes home with a bagful of small-mouthed bass.

Jeannie C. Riley. Brentwood, Tennessee. Jeannie's bus is a $100,000 custom-made Silver Eagle. It's as sumptuous inside as the living room of her home near Nashville.

The singer of "Harper Valley P.T.A.," which sold more than 4,800,000 singles, reclines on her luxurious couch.

Webb Pierce. Nashville, Tennessee. About three thousand people a week
come by Webb Pierce's house to see his guitar-shaped swimming pool. It's
one hundred feet long, the neck forty feet, the body sixty. It cost about fifty
thousand dollars.

Barbie Benton and Hugh Hefner. Nashville, Tennessee. One of the stars of the Hee Haw show, Barbie has carved herself a career as a country singer, with the help, of course, of her famous benefactor.

Gunilla Knudsen and Barbie Benton. Nashville, Tennessee. They may be romping in a corn patch, but this one is on the set of Hee Haw. Well, that's country dream livin'!

Buck Owens. Bakersfield, California. Owens is in his plush office.

Susan Raye. Bakersfield, California. She's in her living room.

National Life acts almost as a corporate guardian to country music. And of course, its motives are not exactly charitable or entirely dedicated to the preservation of an American heritage. Its executives understood a long time ago how important it was for its insurance salesmen, hawking their wares throughout the Midwest and South, to be able to knock on any door and identify themselves with the Grand Ole Opry.

But National Life's grip on country through the Opry has diminished in recent years as the newer stars emerged and found that membership in the Opry was not as vital to a career as it had once been. The country-music community is no longer as closed today. In earlier days outsiders were admitted only after the most careful scrutiny, and almost everybody who was in any way connected with the business was known to everybody else. In those days, and this is only ten years ago, if a star caught his finger in a car door, the whole community would know about it within twenty-four hours. It was the kind of community where people sent get-well cards for tonsillitis. It's still a battle for the newcomer even today, only less so, but you could still offend fifty people simply by upsetting one prominent member of the clan.

Hank Williams, Jr., once told me that "there was a time when I knew everybody in this business." I believe him.

If this caution toward outsiders seems hard to understand, it must be remembered that country music and country singers suffered for a long time the sneers of the city sophisticates. Often, of course, those sneers were from ex-country people, doing their best to disguise their origins by putting down the music that was too close a reminder of home and its inevitable connotations of poor and rural. This scorn bred a lingering inferiority complex in the country-music community, a complex that still persists somewhat today. It was exacerbated when, in the fifties and sixties, many country performers tried their luck in the centers of sophistication only to find that their indigenous music was ranked a few steps below the likes of entertainers who revolve around the Frank Sinatra/Sammy Davis, Jr., axis. There have never been too many country stars showing up in Earl Wilson's column.

Bill Anderson in his elegant den. Old Hickory Lake, Tennessee.

Connie Smith. Nashville, Tennessee. "I don't think I could have lived the last five and a half years if I hadn't found God," she says.

Brenda Lee. Nashville, Tennessee. She was sixteen years old when she first hit it big in rock 'n' roll with "I'm Sorry." Now she's a country star.

So life in Nashville's music world is still fairly insular. But it's insularity combined with opulence. It's a sugar-and-spice life where country dreams have come true, a world in which the TV commercial has become reality, where folks really do bring tears to daughter's eyes with a new little Vega, where people really do drink mint juleps under willow trees and barbecue chicken on the long summer evenings and nobody gets splashed with grease. It's all come a long way from West Virginia.

# 5
## Good Ole Boys
(and a Few Good Ole Gals)

Don't ask for definitions of a good ole boy. If you don't recognize one when you meet one, you probably never will. You'll just have to take a Southerner's word for it when he tells you, "So and so's a good ole boy."

For myself, I never heard a better definition of a good ole boy than the one advanced by a Texas friend of mine, Dave Hickey, a writer who has written his fair share about the world of country music. Hickey said: "A good ole boy is a man who still gets turned on full blast by ladies who wear their hair in beehives."

Paul Hemphill, author of Nashville Sound, the first major critical work written about country music, recently wrote another series of essays entitled Good Old Boys. In it he lamented the transformation of Southerners as the K-Mart mentality took hold, as America became homogenized, as folks moved to the suburbs and began driving shiny new cars in place of Ford pickup trucks. In another part of his book Hemphill also noted a parallel change in musical tastes, Glen Campbell being preferred to Ernest Tubb, the latter supposedly being too tacky for the emergent middle class. He comes down pretty hard on this trend, remembering a time when the unaffected good ole boy was the very backbone of country-music fans, a time when the stars were good ole boys too, singers who never bothered to learn any fancy patter to precede their act but just came out on stage, planted their feet down firmly and sang.

Well, the good ole boy may be a dying or changing breed, but there's still a good few in country music (plus a few good ole gals, too). And they still provide the very basic style that is real country. When Ernest Tubb or Hank Snow walks out on to the stage of the Opry and sings "Walking the Floor over You" or "Movin' On," the respective hits with which each is instantly identified, a tremor may still be felt through the audience. Neither Tubb nor Snow indulges in any of the fads peculiar to show business which have prompted many country singers to move

---

(Over) The Willis Brothers (Guy, Skeeter and Vic). Opryland, Tennessee. They were the first group to back Hank Williams, which is some sort of Music City milestone.

Skeeter Willis at his locker backstage at the new Opry House.

with the times. Tubb still wears his cowboy hat, and Snow still adorns himself in his rhinestone suit and toupee. Both simply stand there composed and deliver their songs. There's no gimmickry attached; they sing straight from the gut, and the fans are well aware of this.

Now these two may be good ole boys, yet they don't seem to have much in common. Snow, who is sixty years old, is a Canadian by birth, hails from Nova Scotia and sings of railroads and even of life on the ocean. He worked as a cabin boy when he was a youngster. Tubb is from Texas, actually gave Snow a big push when he persuaded him to try out for the Grand Ole Opry and might be called the Last Cowboy, for when he plays in front of a Texas audience, there are few finer sights of fans responding to a singer.

In other words, their backgrounds are about as different as they could be in terms of origin, but it might be hard to find a country-music fan who liked one and didn't like the other. For they share a kindred spirit that reaches right across these United States and represents itself in a vast array of similar views and feelings—the hardness of life; a distaste for institutions, associations, governments; a true love for the country; an admiration for success and singleness of purpose and at the same time a healthy respect for time spent spinning yarns on back porches.

The photos in this chapter cover a wide range of stars of varying ages, degrees of fame and fortune, musical styles and life-styles. Some hail from the old South, the mythical South, with its Rhett Butlers and Scarlett O'Haras, broken-down shacks, cottonfields and good manners. Others are from the new South with its Chrome and Plastic future, freeway interchanges, new cities, toned-down racism. But what they have in common is still strong enough to withstand the strides of progress.

As I said earlier, that common bond is hard to define. It would be self-evident if you saw Jerry Reed and Freddy Hart in the same pickup. It would be quite apparent if you went to a stock-car race with Mel Tillis and Chet Atkins. It would be immediately recognizable if you watched Charlie Rich and Faron Young share a bottle of moonshine. And this camaraderie, which springs from a sense of sameness, is as evident among the fans, the nonstars from the ranks of which these stars have sprung. In the line at the Opry you will see that recognition as

Patsy Montana. Nashville, Tennessee. Patsy was the first female country singer to record a song that sold more than a million copies: "I Want to Be a Cowboy's Sweetheart," recorded in 1936. She's also considered one of the best yodelers in country-music history.

an upstate New York family opens up a dialogue with a couple from Arkansas: "Where y'all from?"

During the social upheavals of the sixties the good ole boy seemed a lot easier to define. He was the emblem of resistance to integration, the supporter of Lester Maddox, the red-faced, rednecked fellow with bushy sideburns and a big belly whose pickup was fitted with a gun rack; he was the united enemy of campus rioters, drug users and war protesters. Now, as the South has been dragged headlong into the twentieth century, there is reason, as Hemphill says, to consider him an endangered species. That old enigmatic Southern character is being sacrificed for a down payment on a color TV. Only, as Larry L. King put it: "I would call a good ole boy a former redneck, except there ain't no such thing."

In other words, there is still some continuity among this confusion. The music of the good ole boys expresses the way they felt yesterday, and it expresses the way they feel today. It is a reminder of what has been and what's been learned. It is a constant in a world whose values have rapidly changed. It has been said that country music grew in popularity because the world of the good ole boy was on the wane and that the new wave was quicker to accept the benefits of technology in recording studios, promotion men and advertising. This may be a partial explanation, but it is secondary to the central truth that the music of the good ole boys, the true country music, lives in the hearts and lives of the people who can respond to it, because it is the story of their lives.

Jean Shepard. Nashville, Tennessee. One of the really big songs of the Korean War was "Dear John Letter," which Jean sang with Ferlin Husky. She was formerly married to Hawkshaw Hawkins, who died in a plane crash in 1963.

Johnny Bond and Pee Wee King. Nashville, Tennessee. Pee Wee is credited with writing "The Tennessee Waltz." Johnny wrote "Cimarron" and starred in hundreds of second-feature westerns as a singing sidekick of Roy Rogers, Gene Autry, Tex Ritter and Hopalong Cassidy.

Hank Snow. Nashville, Tennessee. "The Singing Ranger" is pictured here on his Rainbow Ranch. His name has come to epitomize the very best in country music.

Lefty Frizzell. Hendersonville, Tennessee. Lefty got his name from Texas Boxing Clubs for a record number of southpaw knockouts. Back in the forties and fifties Frizzell was as big a star as any in country and Western. His best-sellers included "Long Black Veil" and "Saginaw, Michigan." He swapped many a line with Hank Williams and heavily influenced Merle Haggard. Tragically, Lefty died shortly after this picture was taken.

Tex Williams. Los Angeles, California. Tex appeared in scores of movies with the late Tex Ritter and Buster Crabbe. He had a huge hit with "Smoke, Smoke, Smoke" in the forties and still makes the charts periodically, as with "The Night Miss Nancy Ann's Hotel for Single Girls Burned Down."

Eddy Arnold with Mickey Mantle. Harpeth Hills, Tennessee. "The Tennessee Plowboy" does not consider himself a country singer yet identifies with the Nashville scene. Now a country gentleman, he has helped bring country up-town by working to "cut out the by-cracky nonsense and give respect to our music; then people will respect us." He was elected to the Country Music Hall of Fame in 1966.

Johnny Russell. Oklahoma City, Oklahoma. Johnny's a heavy man who became a lot heavier after his big 1973 hit "Rednecks, White Socks and Blue
Ribbon Beer."

Brenda Lee and her daughter. Nashville, Tennessee.

Chet Atkins. Harpeth Hills, Tennessee. Called Mr. Nashville, Chet Atkins is one of the most powerful men in country music—ace guitarist, vice-president of R.C.A. Records and the founder of countless other country-music careers. "If Chet likes it," it is often said, "it'll sell."

Jerry Reed. Nashville, Tennessee. A protege of Chet Atkins, Jerry hails from
Georgia, and there's no one faster on the guitar.

Charlie Rich. Benton, Arkansas. Charlie is shown in these photographs with C. J., the old black man who taught him to play and sing the blues. C. J. says of Charlie's father, a plantation foreman in Benton, Arkansas, where Charlie grew up, "There wasn't no man who could sing the blues better than that man." Rich languished in the wilderness for many years, switching record labels, nearly hitting it big several times with SUN Records in the fifties, until he recorded his monster hit, "Behind Closed Doors," and followed it up with the equally lyrical "Most Beautiful Girl."

Charlie Rich is shown after spending a night on a mountain near Colt, Arkansas, where he was born.

Kenny Price. Nashville, Tennessee.
Kenny is known affectionately in the
Nashville music world as the Round
Mound of Sound.

Grandpa Jones, Kenny Price and Buck Trent in the commissary at Hee Haw.
Nashville, Tennessee.

Jerry Clower. Oklahoma City, Oklahoma. He gave up a career as a fertilizer salesman when his friends convinced him to make an amateur recording of his Mississippi yarns. The recording reached Decca, and Clower was off to a huge career as a comic. He's maybe the best Southern storyteller since Willie Morris.

Tennessee Ernie Ford. Nashville, Tennessee. His trademark opening, "Howdy, pea-pickers," is familiar to generations of country fans. Here he returns to Nashville from his country-music tour of the Soviet Union.

Hank Thompson. Tulsa, Oklahoma. For years his band, the Brazos Valley Boys, was one of the most popular in country and Western. A champion of Western swing, Hank kept 'em dancing through the fifties. Bob Dylan has claimed Thompson as one of his major influences.

Roy Clark (with Diana Trask). Tulsa, Oklahoma. Roy's phenomenal success in recent years has brought him the C.M.A. Entertainer of the Year Award and helps him to support two airplanes, three racehorses, two boats, two motorcycles, four children, a wife and Buck Trent.

Earl Scruggs. Madison, Tennessee. The virtuoso banjo picker now works with his three sons, along with Jody Maphis and Josh Graves. He calls the group a "no-cubbyhole, category-free, barrierless approach to music." His new album attracted many superstars as sidemen. It was the first country super-session album.

Freddie Hart. Nashville, Tennessee. With a second-grade education and a fourth-degree black belt in karate, Freddie Hart says, ''I believe in singing, not fighting.'' Like many other stars, he spent a long time paying dues before his big hit song, ''Easy Lovin'.''

Mel Tillis. Tulsa, Oklahoma. His stutter has been the butt of millions of jokes on the stage of the Opry. Tillis uses it as part of a "comic" portion of a well-choreographed show.

Billy "Crash" Craddock. Nashville, Tennessee. His nickname stems from his interest in football. He began his singing career in 1958, and after numerous ups and downs was rediscovered, you might say, and brought back to Nashville.

Faron Young. Harpeth Hills, Tennessee. Sometimes called the King of the State Fair Circuit. His biggest hit among many big hits was "Hello, Walls."

Karen and Onie Wheeler. Mt. Juliet, Tennessee. Here they're caught in a moment of exuberance.

Charlie McCoy. Nashville, Tennessee. Charlie is the sideman of sidemen, the harp player to end all harp players!

Glen Campbell. Lake Tahoe, Nevada.

Glen Campbell with his mom and dad, a country couple from the town of
Delight, Arkansas. Here they mimic the three monkeys "See No Evil, Hear
No Evil, Speak No Evil," though Glen has been known to roar a little now and
again.

Roger Miller. Lake Tahoe, Nevada. Loving and warm when he wants to be, frenetic and hostile when he feels that way, he's left his mark on Nashville by writing some incredible songs and building the King of the Road Motel (named after his most famous hit).

# A Note from the Photographer

People continually ask me why I, an apparently unlikely candidate, ever ventured to undertake a project involving country music. I suppose the reasons are two-fold. First, although country musicians have had their pictures taken a zillion times, I felt that they had never been photographed, particularly from any cohesive or consistent point of view. And second was the specter of living in the South as I dreamed it: a strange amalgam of Scarlett O'Haras, rednecks, Blanche DuBois, cowboys, weeping willows, fiddles and banjos, y'alls and mint juleps. I suspected that there might be real honest-to-God people living in those romantic Southern hinterlands, but they inhabited a real world then invisible to the ramblings of my imagination. In short, I was intrigued, and I was curious.

Apart from my friend Peter McCabe, the writer of this book, Bonnie Garner, of Columbia Records in Nashville, and my editor, Elisabeth Jakab, my initial announcement of my intention to do this book was met with a form of polite derision all around. In the North friends snickered, wondering why I could possibly be interested in a subject of such irrelevance. In the South my project was met with discreet skepticism; my presumption was vilified. Who was I, after all? I discovered that the Civil War still rages, though very politely these days, even amicably. The final existence of this book is a testimony to the fact that extreme patience and humanity can sometimes triumph over prejudice and generalized hostility.

151

For these purposes my camera served as bridge; it got me from where I was, a girl with interesting intentions, to where I wanted to be. For example, imagine calling up Porter Wagoner and saying, "Hi, I'd like to meet you today!" I guarantee that you would not. But call him up and say, "Hi, I'm here in Nashville doing an important photography book about the most terrific people in country music, and of course I absolutely must include you!" and you might get to meet him. Not necessarily. But you might. At least your chances are a little bit better anyway.

The camera is also a terrific tool for creating what might be called the instant relationship, here exactly relatable to instant rice or instant pudding or instant turkey stuffing. What usually takes a long time happens quickly. Perhaps it's not quite as good, but it suffices. In the photographic situation two people can meet, get to know each other almost intimately and then part, all within ten minutes. I firmly believe the people do know each other, the camera truly being, like the alchemist's stone, a means of revelation if used correctly. It is hard to hide from it, and it is equally hard to hide behind it. If a shooting has been a good one, I always feel exhausted when it is over. And I never leave a shooting feeling indifferent.

Usually a person has a different sense of what they look like or what they are than I do, particularly show business people, who are ultraconscious of their "image." For this reason it is extremely difficult ever to take a picture of a person which they like; they feel they "don't look good" or "photograph badly" or, worst of all, that the photographer is "bad." But taking a picture that a person likes is not always necessarily the aim; sometimes it is more important to take a picture that is true. Like an old-time daguerreotype that took at least twenty minutes to expose in the brightest sunlight and revealed the true characteristic expression of the poor subject whose smile or artifice could not be sustained for so long, so it can be with a photo session. Be careful to be honest, and a person today will just as surely be revealed for what he or she is before a probing and uncompromising camera. Fortunately for everyone, there is a commonly inhabited land that lies somewhere between artifice and "truth." Take my picture of Freddie Hart that appears in this book; now, I know that Freddie would prefer to see himself

152

smiling, yet I saw him as sensitive, contemplative. Will he see this picture as "bad," I as "true" and someone else as "beautiful"?

I like to think that this is a book about people who happen to be country-music stars. And photographing a country-music star is not as easy as one might think unless one is willing to rely on gimmicks like flashy nudie suits and hokey props to substitute for revelation in a picture. Because without those things, your typical country star looks like your typical Nashville suburbanite. In the South, after all, all the women want to look like Dolly Parton, with her improbable mountains of long blonde hair, and all the men do look like George Jones. What I tried to reach for was the person, to make it possible for you to meet the same human being that I met that day.

I like to photograph famous people—because I'm always fascinated both by what makes them so different and by what makes them the same as everybody else. I don't really like to take pictures of freaks which make them look freaky, of Southerners which make them look corny, of actors which make them look heroic, because it appears to me then that I have fallen victim to their conceit or to some private joke they are perpetrating which has nothing to do with me. When I do do this, which can be great fun, admittedly, I feel more like a historian or a cataloger than a photographer. I prefer to think, What do I feel about this person and what will he allow me to experience? My favorite people are the ones who allow me to experience a touch of them—their pain, whimsy, joy, madness or whatever while I am with them. I like to meet their muse. It makes good pictures.

Take Jerry Lee Lewis, "The Killer," for example. He's a three-ring circus without any help. When he's in the vicinity, things begin to crackle; when he's present, things pop. One of the most contradictory people I've ever met, he entertains ideas of Godliness, Kindness, Peacefulness and Respect concomitant with passions of the most raucous, violent, irrational, unpredictable nature. Jerry Lee insisted I hang around for three days, without sleeping, flying around on his plane to gigs, drinking, partying, before he'd let me take a picture. He wanted me to know who I was photographing . . . first. It was torture. I was a wreck. But it was fascinating. And it was worth it.

153

Or take Charlie Rich, "The Silver Fox," a man haunted by the double demons of ambition and paranoia. At no time were these conflicting characteristics more apparent than upon the occasion of our visit to the home of C. J., a shack on the Arkansas cotton plantation where Charlie grew up which belongs to the man who taught him to play the blues. The day began with a torrential rainstorm, which seemingly miraculously cleared the moment C. J.'s shack came into view. The weather, in retrospect, was an omen, for Charlie in the course of that day passed again and again from stormy and painful introspection to sunny and cheery optimism. At one moment he appeared overjoyed to see C. J., the next, sorry. At one moment proud of his success, at the next, regretful. Sorry for C. J.'s poverty and simple, immobile life, then envious. One moment happy, the next, depressed. Sometimes he appeared enthusiastic about having his picture taken, suggesting I photograph this or that, posing here and there—a moment later, occasionally a second later, he became angry if I even pointed my camera in his direction. As the sun went down after a long, emotional and even traumatic day, Charlie turned to me and said, "You wanted the Charlie Rich story! Well, you're going to get the whole Charlie Rich story!" and off we whisked to a mountaintop in Colt, Arkansas, where Charlie was born. There his double demons emerged claws bared, and I watched helplessly while they tortured him for the rest of that night. I did meet his muse. I did take good pictures. And I emerged from that experience with a vision of stardom I'd never had before.

As you can see, I prefer to take pictures of people who are moving than portraits of people who are still, posing. In the portrait one is most aware of what a person looks like, the light, the composition of the picture. In a photograph of a person moving, doing something, one becomes aware not only of the same elements as in the portrait but of the additional element of what that person might be like. Lighting and composition become the tools, rather than the result, of one's work.

For this book I used two Nikon F bodies, one motorized Nikon F2 body, and 28, 35, 50, 55 micro, and 135 mm Nikkor lenses. I used mainly Kodak Plus-X and some Kodak Tri-X film. All the pictures were printed on Agfa Brovira paper.